Journeys: Land, Air, Sea

Understanding Grid Coordinates

Moira Anderson

Publishing Credits

Editor
Sara Johnson

Editorial Director
Emily R. Smith, M.A.Ed.

Editor-in-Chief
Sharon Coan, M.S.Ed.

Creative Director
Lee Aucoin

Publisher
Rachelle Cracchiolo, M.S.Ed.

Image Credits

The author and publisher would like to gratefully credit or acknowledge the following for permission to reproduce copyright material: cover,123rf; p.1, Corbis, p.4, The Photo Library/Alamy; p.4 (inset), Alamy; p.5, Newspix (inset); p.5, The Photo Library/Alamy; p.6, Getty Images; p.8, Mapping Specialists, Ltd.; p.9, Shutterstock; p.10 (top), The Photo Library/Science Photo Library; p.10 (bottom), Shutterstock; p.13, The Photo Library; p.14, © Airservices Australia; p.15, Newspix; pp.16-17, The Photo Library/ Mary Evans Picture Library; p.18, The Photo Library/Alamy; p: 19, Shutterstock; p.20, The Australian Hydrographic Service (Certain material in this product is reproduce under licence by permission of The Australian Hydrographic Service. © Commonwealth of Australia 2008. All rights reserved. This information may not be copied, reproduced, translated, or reduced to any electronic medium or machine readable form, in whole or part, without the prior written consent of the Australian Hydrographic Service); p.21, The Photo Library; p.22, The Photo Library; p.22 (inset), The Photo Library/Science Photo Library; p.23, Alamy; p.24, Shutterstock; p.25, The Photo Library/ Bridgeman Art Library; p.27, Corbis. Illustrations on pp. 6, 7, 11, 12, 16, 19, 23, 26, and 28 by Lewis Chandler.

While every care has been taken to trace and acknowledge copyright, the publishers tender their apologies for any accidental infringement where copyright has proved untraceable. They would be pleased to come to a suitable arrangement with the rightful owner in each case.

Teacher Created Materials

5301 Oceanus Drive
Huntington Beach, CA 92649-1030
http://www.tcmpub.com

ISBN 978-0-7439-0900-6
© 2009 Teacher Created Materials, Inc.
Reprinted 2013

Table of Contents

Using Maps

People have used maps for thousands of years. We are still using maps today. Maps help us to plan **journeys**. Maps help us get to places. They can even show us where we are if we get lost.

☐ Using a map in a shopping mall

♦ A map to help hikers

Many people use maps as part of their jobs. There are maps for journeys over land. There are maps for journeys in the air or on the sea. Let's take a closer look at these different types of maps.

Pilots use charts for air journeys ◆

Charts Are Maps, Too

Maps have different names depending on whether they are used for land, air, or sea. In the air or at sea, a map is known as a chart.

❑ **A sea chart**

Land: Street Maps

Many people use street maps at work. Couriers carry goods. Taxi drivers take people to places. Ambulance drivers take people to hospitals. Street maps help these people find the best **routes** to take.

Look at this street map. Which route would you take from City Park to the hospital? ◆

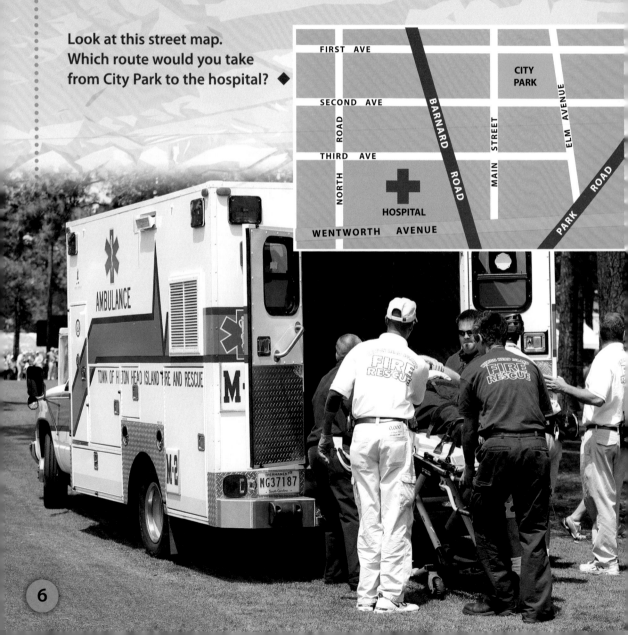

Street maps have horizontal and vertical lines on them. These lines cross and form a grid of cells. Each cell has a letter and a number. This letter and number is called a grid coordinate. Grid coordinates help people find places.

What will you locate at the grid coordinate C2? First, locate the letter C and then locate the number 2. Now, locate the cell where these coordinates cross. You find Central Park.

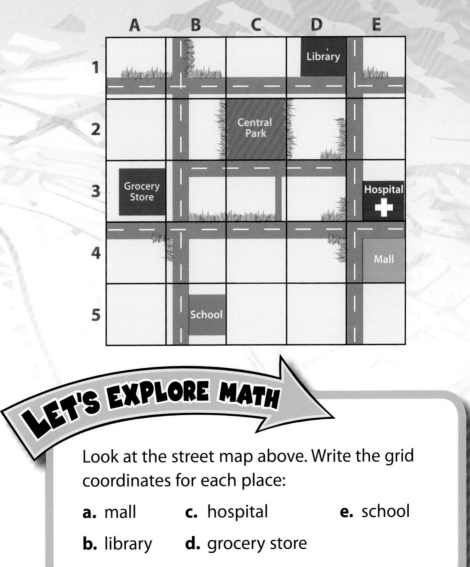

LET'S EXPLORE MATH

Look at the street map above. Write the grid coordinates for each place:

a. mall   **c.** hospital   **e.** school

b. library   **d.** grocery store

Land: Road Maps

Road maps may show larger areas than street maps. Like street maps, road maps have grid coordinates. Road maps also have **keys**. The key shows little pictures called **symbols** (SIM-buhls). Each symbol stands for something on the map.

Key:

★ State capital

5 — Interstate highway

395 — US highway

58 — State highway

- - - - - State boundary

PACIFIC OCEAN

CALIFORNIA

Sacramento · 80 · 99 · 50 · 95 · 395 · Mono Lake · 6 · Oakland · San Francisco · 580 · 120 · Modesto · 6 · San Jose · 395 · 101 · 5 · Monterey · Salinas · 99 · Fresno · Lone · 41 · 101 · 99 · Bakersfield · San Luis Obispo · 58 · 5 · 101 · Santa Clarit · Santa Barbara · 10 · Los Angeles

N

0   200 miles
0   200 kilometers

Truck Drivers

Truck drivers use road maps to plan their trips. They use a map's scale to work out distances. A map's scale is written as a **ratio**. A ratio is a comparison of 2 numbers. So on a map, the scale may be 1:20. This means that 1 inch equals 20 miles of distance.

❑ **Truck drivers can travel hundreds of miles to deliver their goods.**

EVADA

6

95

Las Vegas

15

40

95

Bernardino

10

Salton Sea

◆ **Road maps show main highways and roads. They show cities and towns.**

Land: GPS

A GPS satellite in space

Some people use a global positioning system (GPS) in their trucks or cars. A GPS uses satellites that orbit Earth. The satellites send signals to GPS receivers. A GPS can show **location** (lo-KAY-shuhn), speed, and direction.

A GPS shows street maps. The street maps show the route to a location. They also show the direction the car is going. As the car moves, the map changes to show its new location.

❏ A GPS being used in a car

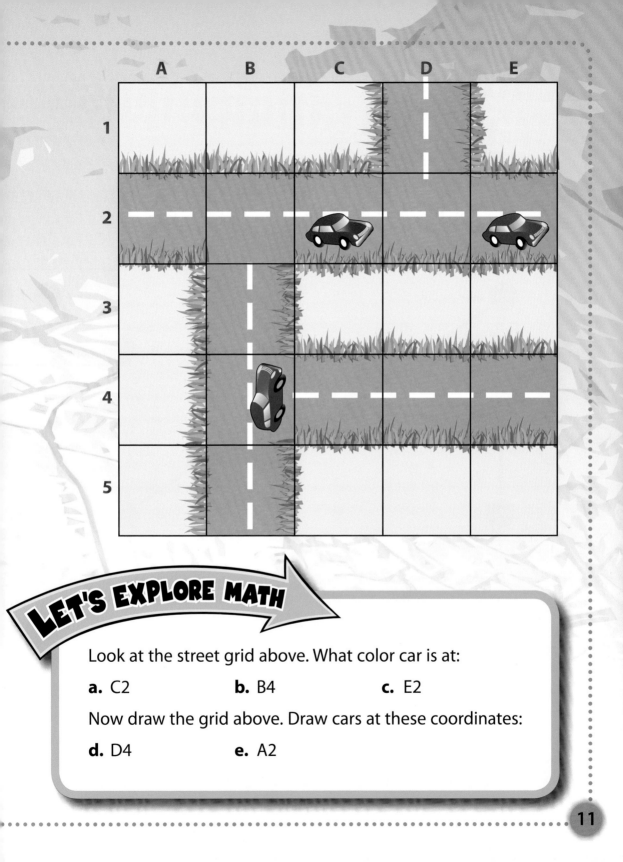

LET'S EXPLORE MATH

Look at the street grid above. What color car is at:

a. C2   **b.** B4   **c.** E2

Now draw the grid above. Draw cars at these coordinates:

d. D4   **e.** A2

Land: Transportation Maps

Some people use public transportation maps to get around a city. Trains and buses have special maps.

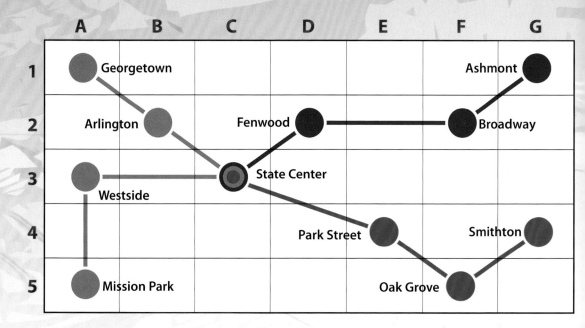

LET'S EXPLORE MATH

Look at the subway map above. Write the names of the stations at the following coordinates.

a. E4   **b.** A5   **c.** D2   **d.** F5   **e.** B2   **f.** G1   **g.** C3

h. What color routes would you take to get from F2 to A3?

i. Explain how you solved problem h.

Air Charts

Airplane pilots use maps to work out their flight routes. These maps are called air charts. These charts show the main **landmarks** on the ground.

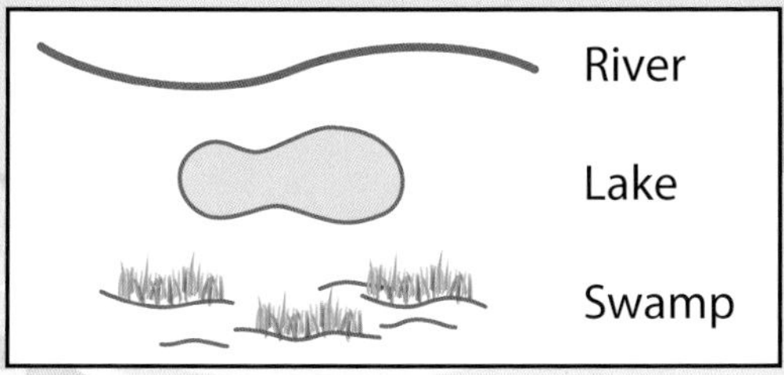

River

Lake

Swamp

◆ Air charts use symbols to show landmarks such as rivers and lakes.

Some air charts cover very large areas. Like street and road maps, air charts are drawn to scale. The air chart below has a scale of 1:500,000! This means that 1 centimeter (0.4 in.) on the map represents about 5 kilometers (3.1 miles) on the land.

❏ **Air charts are very detailed. This is an air chart of Melbourne, Australia.**

Air: GPS

Today, nearly every airplane has a GPS. The GPS helps the pilot see where the plane is. It also shows how high the plane is flying. And the GPS can show distance between locations.

GPS in an airplane ❑

An Amazing Journey

In 1927, Charles Lindbergh flew alone, nonstop across the Atlantic Ocean. He was the first pilot to make this trip. Lindbergh flew for 33 hours. He traveled 3,610 miles (5,810 km).

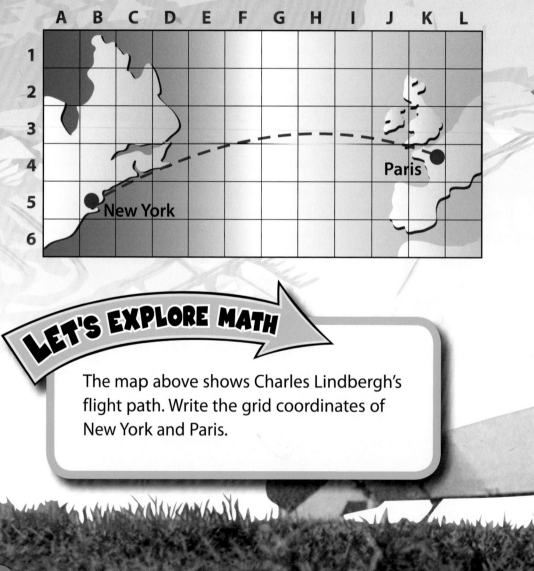

LET'S EXPLORE MATH

The map above shows Charles Lindbergh's flight path. Write the grid coordinates of New York and Paris.

Lindbergh did not have a map. He did not have a GPS. An instrument on the plane showed how fast he was flying. Lindbergh used a **compass**, and he could only estimate where he was.

♦ Charles Lindbergh's plane is called *Spirit of St. Louis*. You can see this plane at the Smithsonian National Air and Space Museum.

Land and Air: Compasses

All airplanes have compasses. So do some cars and trucks. A compass is a tool that shows **direction** (duh-REK-shuhn). Compasses help people know which direction they are traveling in.

compass

Compass Points

The main points on a compass show north, south, east, and west. A compass rose on a map shows north. This helps you figure out which direction to travel.

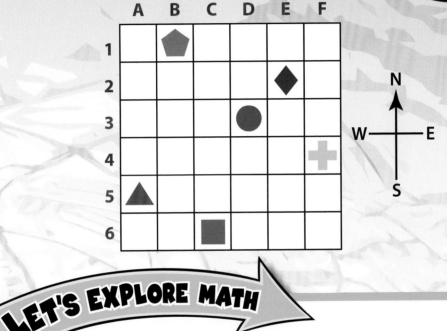

LET'S EXPLORE MATH

Use the compass rose and grid to answer these questions. Write the grid coordinates for each answer.

a. Which shape is north of B6?

b. Which shape is west of D6?

c. Which shape is east of C3?

d. Which shape is south of A3?

e. Which shape is north of E6?

f. Which shape is east of D4?

Sea: Charts

   People who sail ships and boats also use maps. These maps are called sea charts. Like other maps, sea charts have keys. They also have compass roses that are **illustrated** (il-luh-STRAH-tuhd) compasses drawn in circles.

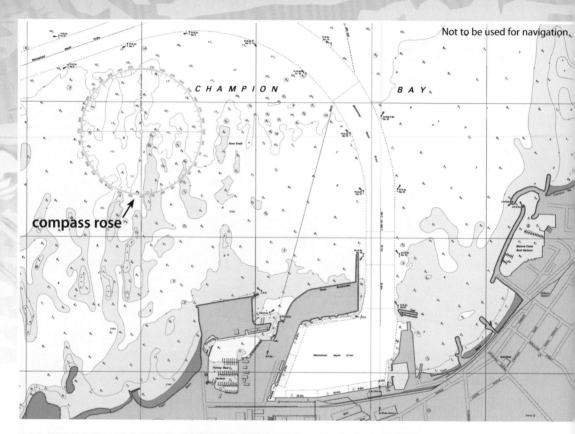

Not to be used for navigation.

compass rose

What Is a Nautical Mile?

A **nautical** (NAW-tuh-kuhl) mile is different than a mile measured on land. One nautical mile is 1.15 miles (1.85 km) on land. Nautical charts have scales that show nautical miles.

Sea charts also show how deep the water is. They show islands and lighthouses. Some sea charts show harbors and bridges, too.

Sea: GPS

Ships also use GPS. A GPS can be used anywhere in the world. The GPS can tell a captain the ship's location. The captain can also use the GPS to work out the distance and directions to a **destination** (dess-tuh-NAY-shuhn).

Radars

Ships also use **radars** to travel. Radars are instruments that find objects. Radars send signals toward an object. The signals bounce back from the object to the radar. The signals show the location of the object and its distance from the ship.

◆ A ship's radar

Sea: Compasses

Most ships and boats also have compasses. Just like compasses on land and in the air, sea compasses also show direction. The points on the compasses help the crew figure out which direction the ships or boats are sailing.

Use the sea chart and compass rose to solve this problem.

Start at D4. Go west to B4.

a. Which island have you landed on?

Now go north from B4 to B1. Go east to D1. Then go south to D2.

b. Which island have you landed on?

c. Write directions from this island to Round Island.

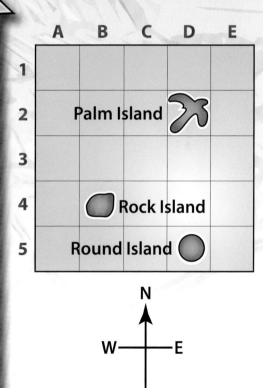

Navigation Long Ago

Long ago, sailors did not use charts. Instead, they often sailed their ships near the land. Landmarks, such as towns or mountains, guided them.

Lighthouses

Lighthouses were very important to ships and boats long ago. When it was dark or the weather was bad, the light from a lighthouse warned captains that they were getting too close to land or rocks.

Sometimes, land was not always in sight. Early sailors used features in the sky to figure out where they were. Sailors could find out their locations using the position of the sun, the moon, and stars. They also used early **navigational** (nav-uh-GAY-shuhn-uhl) instruments.

Space: Moon Maps

Today, maps are even made of the moon. An instrument orbits the moon, measuring its hills and craters. This information is then made into a map.

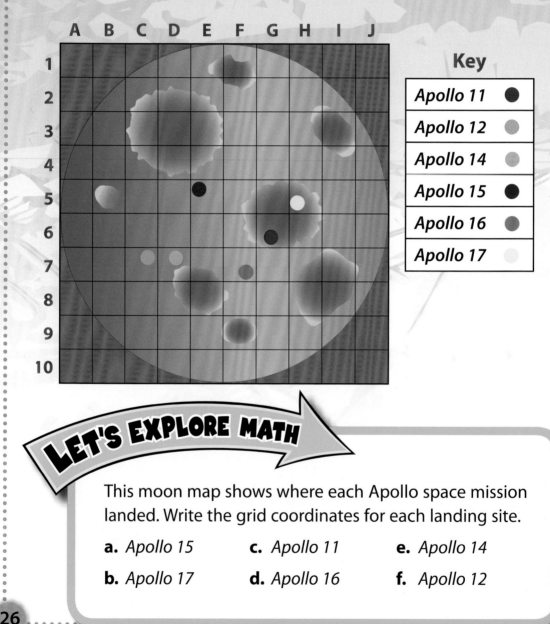

Key	
Apollo 11	●
Apollo 12	●
Apollo 14	●
Apollo 15	●
Apollo 16	●
Apollo 17	●

LET'S EXPLORE MATH

This moon map shows where each Apollo space mission landed. Write the grid coordinates for each landing site.

a. *Apollo 15* **c.** *Apollo 11* **e.** *Apollo 14*

b. *Apollo 17* **d.** *Apollo 16* **f.** *Apollo 12*

Maps Every Day

Maps are used by people every day. Some people use maps in their jobs. Other people use maps to go on vacation. Others use maps to take a bus across town. Maps are really useful. Where would we be without maps?

Getting Home

This is a street map of Sierra's town. Today, Sierra will visit each location on her way home from school. First, she has to run some errands for her mom. She also wants to meet her friends at the playground. Last, Sierra has a swimming lesson.

The map of Sierra's town is shown below on a coordinate plane. A coordinate plane is a lot like a grid map. It has labels, horizontal and vertical lines, and sections. But coordinate planes are labeled on the lines, not the spaces. The point is labeled where 2 lines cross. Most of the time, coordinate planes use only numbers to label the lines. For example, on the map below, the library is on point (5, 6).

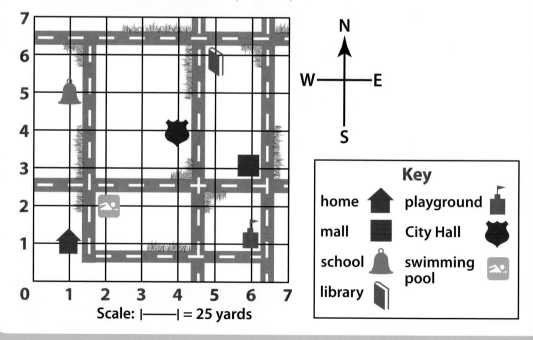

Scale: |———| = 25 yards

Key

home	🏠	playground	🟦
mall	⬛	City Hall	🛡
school	🔔	swimming pool	🏊
library	📖		

Solve It!

a. Write the grid coordinates and approximate compass directions for a route Sierra could take.

b. Work out the distance Sierra traveled on this route.

Use the steps below to help you explain the route you chose for Sierra.

Step 1: Plan Sierra's route. Write the grid coordinates for each location in the order in which Sierra will visit them.

Step 2: Use approximate compass directions (north, south, east, west) to describe the route Sierra took. For example, start at (1, 5) head east to (5, 5).

Step 3: Use the scale to work out approximately how far Sierra traveled.

Is There Another Way?

c. Is there a different route Sierra could take that covers a shorter distance?

Glossary

compass—an instrument used to show direction

destination—the place that is the end of a journey

direction—the line or route in which something is moving, facing, or pointing

illustrated—drawn, not photographic

journeys—traveling from one place to another

keys—lists that explain symbols used in a map

landmarks—easy to recognize and obvious objects in a landscape

location—the point, position, or place in which someone or something is

nautical—relating to ships, and customs and practices people follow at sea

navigational—relating to steering and controling the course of something, such as ship, airplane, or car

radars—instruments that send out radio waves as a way of finding the position of objects

ratio—a comparison of two quantities; one amount is a fraction of the other

routes—paths taken to get from one place to another

symbols—letters or simple pictures that have widely recognized meanings

Index

Let's Explore Math

Page 7:

a. E4   **b.** D1   **c.** E3   **d.** A3   **e.** B5

Page 11:

a. red   **b.** blue   **c.** brown   **d.** Check student work.   **e.** Check student work.

Page 12:

a. Park Street   **d.** Oak Grove   **g.** State Center
b. Mission Park   **e.** Arlington   **h.** Blue and red routes
c. Fenwood   **f.** Ashmont   **i.** Answers will vary.

Page 16:

New York: B5; Paris: K4

Page 19:

a. pentagon   **b.** square   **c.** circle   **d.** triangle   **e.** diamond   **f.** cross

Page 23:

a. Rock Island   **b.** Palm Island   **c.** Go south to D5.

Page 26:

a. E5   **b.** H5   **c.** G6   **d.** F7   **e.** D7   **f.** C7

Problem-Solving Activity

a. Answers will vary but should include grid coordinates and compass directions.

b. Answers will vary depending on the route chosen.

Sample Route

Step 1:   School: (1, 5); Library: (5, 6); City Hall: (4, 4); Mall: (6, 3); Playground: (6, 1);
Swimming: (2, 2); Home: (1, 1).

Step 2:   (1, 5) head east to (5, 5). Head north to (5, 6). Then head south to (5, 4). Go west
to (4, 4). Then go south to (4, 3). Head east to (6, 3). Head south to (6, 1). Then head
west to (2, 1). Head north to (2, 2). Head west to (1, 2). Then head south to (1, 1).

Step 3:   (1, 5) head east to (5, 5) = 100 yards. Head north to (5, 6) = 25 yards.
So school to library = 125 yards.
(5, 6) head south to (5, 4) = 50 yards. Head west to (4, 4) = 25 yards.
So library to city hall = 75 yards.
(4, 4) go south to (4, 3) = 25 yards. Head east to (6, 3) = 50 yards.
So city hall to mall = 75 yards.
(6, 3) head south to (6, 1) = 50 yards.
So mall to playground = 50 yards.
(6, 1) head west to (2, 1) = 100 yards. Head north to (2,2) = 25 yards.
So playground to swimming pool = 125 yards.
(2, 2) head west to (1, 2) and south to (1, 1) = 50 yards.
So swimming pool to home = 50 yards.

125 yards + 75 yards + 75 yards + 50 yards + 125 yards + 50 yards = 500 yards. Sierra traveled
500 yards.

c. Answers will vary.